A GUIDE TO THE
JUVENILE JUSTICE SYSTEM

A GUIDE TO THE JUVENILE JUSTICE SYSTEM

FRED HENDRICKS

This book and all interpretations or definitions of laws, codes and organizations are the opinion of the author and not to be used as legal advice.

Definitions and interpretations were taken from the Penal Codes, Health and Safety Codes and Welfare and Institution Codes.

This book or parts thereof may not be reproduced in any form, stored in a retrieval system, or transmitted in any form by any means-electronic, mechanical, photocopy, recording, or otherwise-without prior written permission of the publisher, except as provided by United States of America copyright law.

ISBN 978-0-557-42499-3

Published by Juvenile Justice Incorporated

This book was written in memory of
Adebayo "Bayo" Adenika
My friend and best martial arts student

Special Dedication

To my wife Rachelle, Thank you for all of your Love and Support

To my children Freddy, Ryan, Genesis, Amere and Abbasi

Dedication

To my parents Robert and Clara Hendricks
and Mrs. Gloria Henry

To my brothers Robert and Michael and cousin Candy

To my very close friends Kapri, Senior Officer Ed Browder,
Officer J.D. Williams, M.C. Crunch
and Frank Gonzalez

TABLE OF CONTENTS

FOREWORD

When I became a police officer, I committed myself to enforcing the laws and arresting the guilty. While working on the campuses of schools throughout Los Angeles, I arrested many young people who did not realize they were committing a crime. In each instance, I told them "Ignorance is no excuse of the law" and took them to jail. My perspective changed when my son asked, "If ignorance is no excuse of the law, who is there to teach us the law?" I realized he was right. There wasn't anyone teaching our children or their parents about the laws that affect their lives and their future.

A Guide to The Juvenile Justice System is written to inform and educate parents and young people about the juvenile justice system. I purposely omitted common police jargon and legal terms as this book is for individuals who have had little or no experience with the legal system. The people who read this book will gain a basic understanding of the juvenile legal system. The laws have become very technical, but the dissemination of the laws and their penalties, unfortunately, do not reach young people until they become a part of the system.

Twenty-five years ago a television show entitled "Scared Straight" was aired. Juvenile offenders were taken to a maximum security prison where inmates with long sentences warned the young offenders about prison life. In one scene an inmate who was serving a life sentence grabbed the juveniles' shoes and threw them across the room. He took another student by the arm and declared that young man now belonged to him. This was designed to shock the juveniles into understanding the harshness and cruelties of prison life. Whether or not this tactic was useful in deterring young people from criminal behavior is not the point. The fact that someone was making an effort to educate—or at least give young offenders a glimpse of prison life—is the issue.

Today our children don't have to go to a prison to see the horrors of the adult criminal system. The juvenile justice system is enough to scare them straight with the existence of racism, cruelty, and degrading and dehumanizing situations. Very few facilities even meet the basic health and educational needs of the juvenile offender.

A Guide to The Juvenile Justice System is written during a time when there is more focus on juvenile punishment than rehabilitation. Today a child in the ninth grade, generally aged 14 or 15, could be sent to an adult courtroom facing adult punishment. In some states children as young as 11 are charged as adults for crimes they committed. A Guide to The Juvenile Justice System is not written to "scare you straight" but to inform you that the original intent of the juvenile justice system was based on rehabilitation not punishment, but that intent has changed over time.

Crimes committed by juvenile offenders have become more violent. For this reason, the juvenile justice system has changed its posture from rehabilitation to punishment for crimes committed, similar to the adult criminal justice system. Although there are more elements of rehabilitation in the juvenile justice system than in the adult criminal justice system, the two systems are becoming increasingly similar. This book will inform parents about their responsibility to teach their children about the laws pertaining to them. Now is the time for parents to empower themselves with information and educate their children. Parents can no longer rely on the school or anyone else to teach their children about juvenile law.

INTRODUCTION

I originally entitled this book the *Black Youth Handbook* because one out of every five African American males goes to jail at some point in his life. I am an African American and have four sons, so those statistics include us. Although we are considered a minority, we are a majority in the prison population. The number of African American men either in jail or on probation or parole is staggering. During a time when crime is declining in the nation, African American men still fill the prisons throughout the country. Latino men are not far behind with their numbers in prison far exceeding their percentages of the total population of this country.

After walking down the halls of the juvenile courts and seeing the faces of bewildered parents and confused young people of all races I asked God to give me the inspiration to write a book that would assist those in need of help and advice. The juvenile justice system is huge and without a clear understanding of what the system is and how it functions, young people destroy their future by making unwise decisions that will alter the rest of their lives. I believe the same amount of money used to lock up young people should be spent on juvenile prevention, but it is not.

Before you arrive at the impression that I am soft on crime, let me reassure you that I am not. I have worked in law enforcement for 20 years. I have seen gang members kill one another and have witnessed senseless violence perpetrated by our young people. I have seen countless young people locked up, some with lengthy sentences.

I decided to become a police officer in memory of an innocent young man who had the potential of doing something phenomenal with his life. He was killed in a drive-by shooting while standing at a bus stop on the way home from his after school job. When I learned of his death, I made a commitment to enter law enforcement and to spend my life working with young people.

This book has several objectives. One of those objectives is to help young people and their parents involved in a system that can be overwhelming and uncaring. After reading this book you will realize the consequences of youth criminal actions and understand the process involved with holding juveniles accountable for those actions.

JUVENILE JUSTICE SYSTEM ORIGINS

The modern day juvenile justice system is less than one hundred years old. Prior to its inception, juveniles over the age of seven were tried as adults and if they were found guilty of a crime, they faced the same sentencing as their adult counterparts, including long imprisonment and death. The initial juvenile justice system was created in the 1800s to help the country set up policies and standards regarding juvenile offenders. Although it was designed to help rehabilitate youthful offenders, they were still treated like adults in many ways. In 1824, early youth advocates built the New York House of Refuge. It was used to house juveniles that would have otherwise been placed in prison. In 1899, individual states began to establish similar facilities. Juveniles were no longer treated like adults and their cases were heard by judges who took into consideration the need to rehabilitate youthful offenders in an effort to keep them from continuing a life of crime as an adult. Although there had been changes in the juvenile justice system, there were no clear guidelines regarding due process for juvenile offenders.

In 1967, a landmark case involving a juvenile named Gerald Gault reached the United States Supreme Court. The case began in 1964, in Gilo, Arizona, when the sheriff went to the house of 15 year old Gerald Gault and arrested him without notifying his parents. Gault was accused of using profanity during a telephone call with an adult female neighbor. Gault's parents believed that his rights were violated from the initial police contact throughout the court proceedings. Eventually Gerald Gault was found delinquent (guilty of the crime) and sentenced to an Industrial School (juvenile facility) until the age of 21. Gault's parents were unsuccessful in their request in the lower courts to get their son released and in 1967, the case was heard by the United States Supreme Court. In an 8-1 ruling in favor of the Gaults, the Supreme Court ruled that Gerald Gault's right to "due process" under the 14th Amendment had been violated.

In 1968, Congress enacted the Juvenile Delinquency and Control Act to help establish the modern day juvenile justice system. It is made up of a set of rules and procedures to be used whenever juveniles are accused of committing a crime. The juvenile justice system is responsible for public safety in the same manner as the adult criminal justice system. It has a responsibility to protect citizens from juveniles that commit crimes harming the public.

The major difference between the juvenile justice system and the adult criminal system is that the juvenile justice system must place rehabilitation before punishment, whereas the adult criminal justice system places punishment for a crime before rehabilitation. The juvenile justice system recognizes that children have a greater chance of being rehabilitated than adults and that age in some instances mitigates behavior.

Because of cases similar to Gerald Gault, the juvenile justice system was considered a failure; and in 1974, Congress passed the Juvenile Justice Delinquency Prevention Act to set procedures and guidelines for states to follow. It listed juveniles as persons under the age of 18; stressing prevention, rehabilitation, training, education, and treatment rather than incarceration. The act removed juveniles from adult jails and prisons.

In the 1970s, the juvenile justice system was what I call a "user friendly organization." The courts focused on the child's best interest as opposed to his or her punishment, which is how the system was designed to work. The emphasis was on juvenile delinquency and the plight of underprivileged children. The major crimes involving juveniles were delinquency and vandalism. Street gangs were in their infancy and hadn't become the violent gangs they are today.

In the 1980s there was a surge of juvenile crimes unlike those in the 70s fueled, in part, by the "crack cocaine" epidemic that hit the inner cities throughout the country. Juveniles were recruited by adult gang members to sell drugs and carry guns because the gang members knew if the police caught the juvenile offenders, the penalties for their crimes would be more lenient than for the adult offenders. These violent juvenile gang members began committing crimes that the juvenile justice system was not prepared to address. They killed each other over drug "turf" and with the money they made selling drugs, many of these gang members became heavily armed and ready to pull the trigger on rival gangs at any time.

The juvenile gangs struck fear in the heart of entire communities. The death toll of these young people still has not been fully rung and the ramification of this violent period has not been fully felt to this day. The perception from the public was that crime was crime regardless of the age of the person committing it. The public outcry over this violence led to the enactment of the "get tough on crime laws" all over the country. These laws were passed to be a deterrent to crime and to strengthen both the adult criminal system and juvenile justice system. Some of these changes made it easier to send juvenile cases to adult courts and dramatically increased the number of juveniles tried as adults throughout the U.S. Currently, every state has some provisions that allow them to prosecute juveniles as adults. The age to prosecute juveniles as adults can range anywhere from 11 to 17.

The juvenile justice system is a huge mixture of police, probation, social workers, youth advocates, and court personnel. Today the juvenile justice system still places rehabilitation as a primary focus but the incarceration of juvenile offenders is easier and continues to increase. Sometimes I am unsure in which direction the juvenile justice system is headed. I have observed cases of it being caring and placing the future of the juvenile offender and his rehabilitation at the forefront. I have also observed cases in which juvenile offenders were rushed to adult court for crimes that 10 years ago would have never left juvenile court.

JUVENILE LAW

Juvenile law is the term used for laws specifically designed to govern the behavior of the population under the age of 18. A few examples of juvenile laws are curfew violations, truancy, consuming and/or purchasing alcohol and purchasing cigarettes. The reason these offenses are juvenile offenses is because they apply only to persons under the age of 18. An adult cannot be arrested for these particular crimes.

Juvenile law is also applied when juveniles are accused of committing common crimes. These are crimes that apply to both adults and juveniles, such as vandalism, burglary, battery, theft, robbery, and murder. Juvenile law contains the procedures by which the parents, police, probation and the court system will handle juveniles accused of violating both common crimes and juvenile law violations.

Juvenile laws have changed as the public perception of crime has changed. Some members of our population continue to believe that violations of the law by juveniles should be administered differently than adults accused of the same violation. Other members of the population have a general disdain for perpetrators of crimes regardless of the age of the offender. Both trains of thought are exhibited in juvenile law. Youth prevention programs and various types of probation programs remain in place to help juveniles rehabilitate. California, which has the largest number of juveniles housed in juvenile facilities, has probation officers on many of the school campuses.

Most states have new "get tough laws," which have increased the punishment for juvenile offenders. In 2002, the voters in California passed Proposition 21. A part of that provision removed the barrier requiring prosecutors to go to a juvenile judge to request that a case be sent to adult court. Without that barrier, prosecutors have sent a larger number of juvenile cases to adult court for stiffer penalties.

In California, 14 is the age required for juveniles who are accused of serious or violent crimes to have their cases transferred to adult courts for trial. Additionally, some crimes previously considered misdemeanors are now felonies and carry a stiffer penalty. The Three Strikes Law in California could apply to juveniles tried as adults and technically a juvenile could receive "three strikes" before reaching 18.

JUVENILE ARREST

Juvenile arrests are similar to adults. Certain safe guards are in place because the person is under the age of 18. The arrest begins when the juvenile is officially charged with a crime, arrested, and taken into custody. The arrest doesn't mean the juvenile is guilty, but it does mean that the police are officially accusing him of a crime and that they have enough evidence for an arrest. Several steps occur when juveniles are arrested. First, they are read their Miranda rights the same as adults. The arrested juvenile is labeled a subject not a suspect as in an adult arrest. The juvenile, if under the age of 14, has to fill out a Gladys R report. This report is given to determine if the subject can distinguish right from wrong. Next, a juvenile arrest report is completed. This report documents whom the arresting officer contacted on behalf of the juvenile.

If the juvenile is over the age of 11 the booking process is similar to that of an adult suspect. A picture and fingerprints will be taken. The nature of the crime will determine if the juvenile will remain handcuffed, placed in a holding cell or supervised but unsecured by restraints.

During the entire booking process juveniles do not come in contact with adult suspects. Once the booking process is completed, the juvenile subject can remain in police custody for a limited time. In California, a juvenile can be held for six hours from the time of arrest. Once that six-hour time limit has elapsed, the juvenile must be released to a parent or guardian, probation officer, social services or transported to a juvenile facility until the first court appearance. A juvenile cannot post bail for her release.

The Welfare and Institutions Code allows a police officer to arrest a juvenile without a warrant if there is probable cause for the following offenses:

- The juvenile is deemed a habitual truant or runaway.

- The juvenile violated a court order.

- The juvenile escaped a group home, camp or other placement center.

- The juvenile has been accused of committing a misdemeanor or felony.

Additionally, these crimes do not have to be committed in the police officer's presence.

A juvenile 14 years or older arrested for a felony is not released until she has signed a written promise to appear (citation/ticket). The parents of the juvenile must also sign the written promise to appear. A juvenile who has been arrested for using a gun while committing a felony must be detained.

JUVENILE COURT ROOM

Juvenile court rooms are designed to be less intimidating than adult court rooms because the person being charged is under 18. The courtroom itself is usually smaller than an adult courtroom. The judge's bench is smaller and closer to the attorney's table. However, juveniles that are accused of serious crimes may be tried in a court room exactly like an adult court room.

The juvenile courtroom is usually confidential and closed to the public with the following exceptions:

- The parents of the juvenile are allowed to remain in the court room.

- The victim is allowed to bring two people and if the victim isn't present he must be notified of the outcome.

- If the petition is sustained (found guilty), the juvenile's school district must also be notified of the outcome.

- The school must be told if it is a felony or certain type of misdemeanor.

- If a juvenile is arrested on a school campus for a crime against another student or employee of that school or school property, the police can share that information with the school district and principal of the school where the juvenile attends.

- If a juvenile is accused of a violent felony crime the police may release the name and description in an attempt to capture her and prevent her from harming the public.

- If a juvenile 14 or older is convicted of certain serious crimes the police can share that information with the public.

JUVENILE JUDGE

The juvenile judge presides over the courtroom and the proceedings as he would in an adult trial. The judge is the most important figure in the courtroom. The juvenile judge makes the determination of guilt or innocence in all juvenile cases brought before him. Most states do not allow jury trials for juveniles.

In many states there are two judges that preside over juvenile cases. In California, there is a judge or hearing officer that presides over Juvenile Traffic Court and another judge that presides over serious and felony cases involving juveniles. I call this Juvenile Superior Court.

The Juvenile Traffic Court Judge presides over juvenile cases that involve all infractions (fine only violations), vandalism, marijuana possession (less than an ounce), most misdemeanors, vehicle code violations, truancy, curfew, trespassing, fare evasion, and loitering.

The Juvenile Traffic Court Judge can impose the following sentences:

- Admonish the minor and take no further action.

- Order probation for the minor up to six months.

- Order the minor to attend school, counseling sessions, traffic school, community service, or complete a drug treatment program.

- Order the minor to pay restitution or a fine.

- Order the minor's driver's license suspended.

The Juvenile Superior Court Judge handles most serious or violent felonies. The Superior Court Judge can impose the following sentences:

- Probation with several conditions. Including attending school, drug testing, house arrest, prohibition of gang activity, unannounced searches, and placement in juvenile hall.

- Formal probation and removal from the residence with placement in a foster home or group home.

- A short term locked facility (Camp Placement Facility in California) for a period of three, six, nine or ten months.

JUVENILE COURT ATTORNEYS

Three types of lawyers may be involved in a juvenile proceeding; the prosecutor, the public defender, and the private attorney. The prosecuting attorney and public defender are attorneys employed by the court. The private attorney is hired to defend the juvenile accused of a crime.

PROSECUTING ATTORNEY

The prosecuting attorney is there to represent the state and the victim's rights. Two types of prosecutors exist. One is there to seek the truth. Although the juvenile is on trial for a crime that both the police and prosecutor believe has been committed, if the prosecuting attorneys find information that will lead to her innocence they will gladly submit that information to the defense attorney or the courts in the interest of justice and assist the juvenile in clearing her name. Many prosecuting attorneys do just that, they follow the truth no matter where it leads. Not all prosecuting attorneys, however; live on the side of justice. The other type of prosecutor determines that the juvenile is guilty. Once he makes that decision he will do everything possible to convict the juvenile. If evidence surfaces to dispute the claims of guilt, he may hide it or attempt to discredit that information. An important point to remember is that the legal system is adversarial; there is a winner and a loser. Some prosecutors are only interested in winning regardless of the cost.

PUBLIC DEFENDER

If a juvenile can not afford an attorney, the state will provide one at no cost. The same is offered to an adult accused of committing a crime. Most public defenders are as ethical as their prosecuting counterparts. They will work hard to ensure that justice is served in the interest of their juvenile client. Good public defenders vigorously investigate the cases they receive. They follow up on leads that could assist in proving a juvenile's innocence. However, as with prosecuting attorneys, all public defenders aren't equal. Many public defenders have tremendous caseloads and may not be able to give the amount of time needed to litigate a case successfully. Some public defenders do not care about the juvenile clients they serve. They view them as a number and are quick to make a deal with the juvenile's freedom whether it is in the best interest of the juvenile or not.

Two key points are important to note in understanding the role of a juvenile defense attorney. The attorney is representing the juvenile not the parents. In many cases the attorney may have little contact with the parents of the juvenile. It is the responsibility of the juvenile and his parents to do everything they can to help the case. Any information that helps prove or substantiates the juvenile's innocence must be turned over to the attorney as soon as possible. If you have witnesses, make sure the public defender has all information for those witnesses. Juvenile public defenders are only as useful as the information you give them.

PRIVATE ATTORNEY

The juvenile and her family have the option of hiring a private attorney to litigate their case. A public defender is assigned to a case by the court; a private attorney is someone you pay for his legal services. The best way to choose a private attorney is by referral. Hire an attorney that has been effective for someone you know. Again, the private attorney becomes limited by the information you do or do not provide. It is essential to provide any and all information to your attorney so that the right decisions can be made.

JUVENILE INCARCERATION

This chapter is directed at juveniles that are already detained in some type of juvenile facility. Your situation is not without hope and there is something I need to share with you. There is an old saying that goes like this, "You can do time or time can do you." If you are incarcerated, why not make the best of it. First educate yourself. Read everything that you can get your hands on, no matter what the topic. That is what Malcolm X did; he was an illiterate drug using thief when he entered the penitentiary, yet he read every book that he had access to and learned a great many things. Malcolm X was both controversial and powerful. He became a great leader and speaker and wrote and published many essays. Dr. Martin Luther King Jr. wrote some of his most profound speeches while in prison.

Nelson Mandela was wrongfully imprisoned but once he was released he became the President of South Africa. All juveniles detained in juvenile facilities must attend school. You can travel the world with a book or the internet. Read, read, and then read some more. Do not waste your time as so many do. Take this opportunity to do a self-evaluation. First, take an honest look at yourself. If you are guilty of the crime don't blame anyone or anything for your incarceration.

Second, think about what you want to do with your life and how you will go about it. Examine your skills and talents and think about the kinds of jobs for which you are qualified. Consider different kinds of jobs; maybe you never thought about nursing, perhaps you want to work in a pet shop, teach children, design homes, cut and style hair, perhaps start your own business. Nothing is impossible. You can do anything you want in this country (provided it is legal). That is what makes this country so great.

As a juvenile there should be support for you, but if there is not, you have to be self-motivated and willing to work very hard. Juveniles who have returned back into the system are those who did not prepare to make the necessary changes; they had no plan of action.

JUVENILE FACILITIES

Several types of juvenile facilities exist throughout the country. Some states have individualized facilities for juveniles. In California, where there are more juveniles housed than anywhere else in the United States, the following facilities exist:

GROUP HOME is a facility that is run by a non-profit organization. It is used to house juveniles that are not sent to locked juvenile facilities but who are not ready to return to their homes.

CAMP is a facility used to house juvenile offenders. Camp is normally used for short-term offenders.

BOOT CAMP is a juvenile facility patterned after basic training used in the army. It stresses strict discipline and physical exercise. Several police departments also have boot camp programs. These boot camps are usually held on weekends and after school. Their enrollment is voluntary.

DIVISION OF JUVENILE JUSTICE (DJJ) /(Formerly California Youth Authority/CYA) is the juvenile justice system's version of an adult prison. Juvenile offenders can be sentenced to a juvenile facility until they are 25 provided they have no problems in the juvenile facility. This differs from state to state and even from county to county. If a juvenile is tried as an adult and convicted, he can legally remain in a juvenile facility until the age of 25 (provided he has no problems). At the age of 25, he will be transferred to an adult prison for the completion of the sentence. He also can be transferred to an adult facility as young as 16.

HALFWAY HOUSES are facilities used to house juveniles temporarily; either prior to being placed in a home or released. Additionally, they can be placed in a halfway house for medical or drug related reasons.

PRISONS house some juvenile offenders. The juveniles are usually housed in a separate area on the grounds of the prison. However, there are some prisons where the juveniles are in contact with adult prisoners.

JUVENILE TRAFFIC COURT

In California, if a juvenile receives a traffic citation, the case is heard in traffic court. Juvenile traffic court usually handles misdemeanors and infractions. As stated in the next section on court etiquette, there are certain rules guiding the court proceedings. The juvenile judge makes the final decision in the case. The penalties in traffic court are usually fines or community service. Juveniles are rarely taken into custody from traffic court. In traffic court the juveniles usually represent themselves; however, they can have an attorney. The defendant who is the most prepared usually wins. Any information you have to prove your innocence has to be brought to court with you. The court does not waste time while you explain why you don't have the documentation necessary for your case or a witness that you can't find. For example, if a juvenile receives a ticket for truancy going to or coming from the doctor, bring a doctor's note to court.

The way the juveniles present themselves has a big influence on the way the judge will view them. If the juvenile has good grades, bring copies of those grades to court. If the juvenile has good attendance, bring a copy of that attendance record to court. Attempt to get a letter on school stationary from a teacher or administrator to speak on the juvenile's behalf. Give the judge as much positive information as possible.

If you cannot get any information to help the case, be prepared to receive a fine or community service. Any contact with law enforcement is serious and if a juvenile receives a ticket she should always show up in court on the specified date and time. Many juveniles think if they do not show up in court that somehow the problem will go away. When they miss their court date without notifying the court or making special arrangements, a warrant is issued for their arrest making the situation much worse.

A misdemeanor warrant will not bring the police to their house, but it remains on file and if arrested again, they could be detained. In certain cases when the juvenile attempts to get a driver's license, there may be an additional fine or the current license may be suspended. In addition, if the juvenile does not appear in court, it ruins any chance of winning the case.

COURT ETIQUETTE

Once the juvenile and the attorney do everything necessary to prepare their case, they wait for their day in court. The case will be heard in a courtroom where the decision regarding guilt or innocence will be determined. There are certain areas of the case that the juvenile has no control over. The judge will hear the case. The defending attorney will present the case. A prosecuting attorney will attempt to convict. The idea is to win and usually the side that wins is the one that is the most prepared. The way you prepare yourself for your court date will have a great effect on the outcome of your case and is generally the most important factor in determining if you are guilty or innocent.

If a juvenile is serious about winning his case, he will want to do everything possible to make the judge view the case in his favor. When someone goes to a party, he dresses a certain way. When a football team plays, the players dress a certain way. The courtroom is no different. The courtroom attire is a suit and tie or a dress, not the fashion of the day. When a juvenile goes to court looking like a gang member, it makes the case much harder to win. The court day begins prior to entering the courtroom. There are few things a juvenile has control over, and one of them is how she decides to dress. Anything other than proper court attire will make your defense much harder to prove. Although judges are supposed to be impartial, they are also human. This is a simple choice that the juvenile and their parents make that can have a positive or negative impression on the judge who is deciding the case.

Once in the courtroom, the way you act is extremely important. The proper way to address the Judge is **"Your Honor."** Nothing else is acceptable, not "Sir" and definitely not "Ma am." If the judge is treated with disrespect, the accused will have problems. The juvenile may even be sent to lockup for Contempt of Court. The juvenile's future is in the judge's hands. The juvenile must do everything within his power to impress the judge who is hearing the case.

The prosecuting attorney's job is to convict. I can't stress this enough. She may say things that people are not going to like or agree with. Understand that if anyone argues with the court representatives, yells out or does anything inappropriate, it is going to hurt the case. In the courtroom, the attorneys speak and the Judge speaks. **No one else says a word**; not the accused and not anyone inside of the courtroom—**period**. If a message needs to be given to the defending attorney, a note can be passed to him.

RACISM

As much as we would like to say that we live in a colorblind society and that racism does not exist, we cannot, because it does. Racism exists in the juvenile justice system just like it does in many other areas. Our juvenile detention facilities, like our adult detention facilities, are full of people of color and racism plays a part in that. White youth receive probation at a greater percentage than African American or Latino (Hispanic) youth for the same offenses. White youth also have a greater chance of receiving a fair trial.

We have all heard the horror stories of the unfair treatment of people of color in the criminal justice system. I need not go into them here. Everyone is not automatically going to be treated unfairly, but you need to understand the reality that minorities are treated more severely than their white counterparts in many cases. Although people of color are called minorities in the United States, they make up the majority of people in our prisons.

FINES

A fine is the monetary punishment placed on a juvenile found delinquent (convicted) of a crime. The judge imposes a fine that must be paid at the time stated in order to avoid additional penalties.

COMMUNITY SERVICE

Community service is a fine of community work as opposed to a monetary fine. When a juvenile offender is convicted of a crime that requires a monetary fine, the court can assign him to community service instead. The court determines the facility in which the work is to be completed and the amount of time the juvenile offender has to complete it. If the juvenile does not complete the community service, the original fine is reinstated with additional penalties.

TRUANCY AND CURFEW

One of the laws that has had a tremendous impact on students, parents, schools and law enforcement is the daytime truancy and curfew law. Curfew laws involving juveniles have been on the books for many years. In recent years, however, these laws have been more rigorously enforced. The exact time curfew begins may vary from city to city but the general time is from 10:30p.m. to 6:00a.m. If a minor is on the streets between those hours without being accompanied by an adult, including going to or coming from the hospital, he could be given a citation or even arrested. The arrest usually consists of receiving a citation with a date to appear in court. First and foremost, it is imperative to know exactly what the juvenile is being charged with. When the charges are known, you can present your case to your attorney who will present it to the court.

Daytime truancy is a big problem for law enforcement. Children should be in school during the day. Many citations are given to young people who are school aged but not in school. Children must be at school during the daytime and at home late at night. These laws were made to help prevent children from becoming victims of crimes or perpetrating them. An added benefit of this truancy law is that it keeps students at school and safe. There is an old saying that "nothing good ever happens after 8:00 p.m." People drink, do drugs and get involved in situations that they would have never imagined if they were not under the influence. Those very situations can get you involved with police officers. Again, you do not want this to happen. Obey the curfew and truancy laws. They protect you.

SCHOOL GRADES

In every court proceeding involving juveniles, their school records will be discussed. The courts will review the grades and any discipline records of the offender. The defense attorney will present the records if they are favorable to the case. On the other side, the prosecuting attorney will use them against the juvenile if the grades and attendance are poor (usually poor grades and poor attendance go hand-in-hand). School records are similar to job employment history for adults. They not only speak to the academics, but also about the juvenile as a person. School discipline records follow the student from school to school in grades K-12. Parents must impress upon their student how important it is to strive for good attendance, excellent grades, and upright behavior in school. These are the three most important things students must do for their future, their parent's future, and for the community as a whole.

SCHOOL IS YOUR EMPLOYER

Your school is your employer. I know this may sound funny to you especially if you don't have any money in your pocket. Now you may ask "How could I work for the school? They don't pay me to go there." You're correct and under normal circumstances the school works for you. The law states that you have a right to an education and it must be provided to you until you reach the age of 18. However, when you're in the juvenile justice system everything involving school is reversed.

As an adult, if I'm accused of a crime, what I do for a living may affect the amount of my bail and possibly have some bearing on my case. For example, if you're a businessman and you're accused of a crime, your bail could be lowered in certain cases. You're not considered a high flight risk because you have ties to the community and they know where you're going to be. The odds of you running away are less. Your position speaks to your character. If you're homeless your bail could be higher because you have nothing to tie you to the community and you could run away and have nothing to lose.

The school is viewed the same way as a job is for adults. In most all cases involving a juvenile, education is discussed. I have seen several cases in which a letter from a teacher could have been the difference between a juvenile going to jail and being released on probation. Think about that the next time you curse out one of your teachers. If you get in trouble, the school will be contacted for information about your character.

SCHOOL IS YOUR EMPLOYEE

It is critical that students take advantage of everything that a school has to offer, whether it is advanced classes, football, or the chess club. The more connected a student is to school, the better the student will perform. You are paying for those services through your tax dollars. Take advantage of them! Research has shown time and again that the longer a person stays in school, any school, the more income he will make over a lifetime. So yes, there will be pay for the student intimately connected to his education. That is why so many people around the world so desperately want a college education. They know they will be paid for it in time and for the rest of their lives. This is certain. Once education is received, it is the one thing that can never be taken away from the students. The knowledge of a particular skill, science or vocation will last them for the rest of their lives.

Finally, if that is not enough to encourage them to continue their education, research has also shown that a student who drops out of high school has a higher percentage rate of being incarcerated as a juvenile and as an adult. The majority of prison inmates do not have high school diplomas.

POLICE

Law enforcement is the number one way a juvenile is introduced to the juvenile justice system. Whenever a youth is arrested for committing a crime, the police play a large role in determining if the juvenile will be released to go home or continue forward in the system. Any juvenile arrested over the age of 11, in most states, is fingerprinted and photographed. Many times they are released to their guardian and ordered back to the police division the following week accompanied by a guardian. They meet with a juvenile detective who will make any number of recommendations from probation to dismissal of charges.

The role the police play in incarcerating the youthful offender is critically important and a young person must be very careful when confronted by a police officer. The main objective is to avoid a situation in which the police need to make contact with you. Think about your actions and the consequences of them before you act. A juvenile must follow the directions as the officer gives them. A simple situation can become complicated quickly when a person does not follow directions and keep quiet. Do not allow situations to escalate. Your attitude, many times, determines the outcome of your contact with the police.

Police officers have the right to stop you and ask you certain questions. They can ask your name and depending on the information that led them to you (probable cause), they can detain you for further questioning. This is the law. The police do not have to explain what they are doing. This is not the time to have an attitude, ask questions, or show off in front of your friends. The idea is to bring all contact with the officer to an end as soon as possible.

MIRANDA RIGHTS

If you are arrested, "you have the right to remain silent. If you give up the right to remain silent, anything you say can be used against you in a court of law. You have a right to speak with an attorney and have him present during questioning. If you so desire and cannot afford one, an attorney will be appointed for you, without charge, before questioning." This means exactly what it says. If you say anything, it **will** be written in the police report and used against you. Some states will not allow the police to Mirandize a juvenile without a parent or guardian present.

In most states, including California, they do not need a parent present to read Miranda rights to a juvenile. If you are accused of a serious crime, it is best to wait for an attorney or until you can speak to your parents. This is not an admission of guilt, it is just being smart. Anyone in law enforcement who is arrested will never speak until they have an attorney present.

Whenever the police arrest (not stop) you, they must read your Miranda rights to you. You have a right not to speak to the police until you talk to an attorney or your parents. You make the final choice if you want to speak to the police prior to speaking with an attorney.

JUVENILE CITE-BACK

In California, cases in which a juvenile is arrested and not detained or ordered to court but released, a parent must sign a cite-back release form. This form states the juvenile is being released into parental custody. The released juvenile is then ordered to return later for an interview with the juvenile detective assigned to the case. The detective has several options. The juvenile could be counseled and released. This means that after the interview with the detective no further law enforcement action is taken. The detective can choose to send the case to court and have a judge make the determination on how to resolve the case. If this occurs the subject could be detained in a juvenile facility until the court date or remain in the custody of the parent or guardian until that date. The detective makes a determination after reviewing the case and the interview. The outcome you want is for the child to be counseled and released. In order for the detective to release the juvenile without any further law enforcement action, he must believe that this is the best outcome for the juvenile and everyone (victim/public) involved. Bring witnesses and any evidence in your defense to the detective. When you are guilty of a crime (or the evidence proves your guilt), you have to accept responsibility for your actions. It is an indication that you are remorseful and less likely to repeat the offense. When the police have enough evidence to convict the juvenile of the crime, this is not the time to tell a lie. If a person lies and the police know that the person is lying, they will proceed with the case.

   Both parents should attend the cite-back interview. This shows the detective that the parents care about the future of their child. Court etiquette and dress are appropriate for your cite-back interview. Remember the way you look to the detective will have a bearing on the way you are treated. If you look like a gang member, don't be surprised if you are treated like one. The detective has two court options. Juvenile traffic court is where juveniles go for minor offenses. This court is similar to those adults go to for traffic violations. If the detective decides the case is more serious, it could be sent to the District Attorney's office for prosecution in juvenile court.

PROBATION DEPARTMENT

The Los Angeles County Probation Department is the largest department of its kind in the world. It was established in 1903, and serves the superior courts. When police officers arrest minors they can only remain in police custody for a certain length of time (six hours in California).

Once that time has elapsed the juvenile must either be released to a parent, guardian, social service agency, or transported to a facility operated by the probation department. Once the probation department takes custody of the juvenile, a probation officer will complete a report and submit a recommendation to the courts. If the juvenile is found delinquent (guilty) and placed on court ordered probation, the probation department would administer and monitor the juvenile's probation requirements. If the juvenile is detained for the crime, he would be housed in any of the juvenile facilities operated by the probation department. If the case is tried in adult court and gets a guilty verdict, the minor would be sent to a probation facility unless sentenced to the state operated Department of Juvenile Justice (formerly California Youth Authority). The juvenile will remain in either facility until old enough to be transferred to an adult prison facility. The key to understanding the probation officer's role in juvenile court is to remember that they are employees of the court. Their recommendation is held in high regard by the juvenile judge and many of the courts decisions are based on the probation officers' recommendation.

The Probation Department must detain a juvenile for the following violations:

- A juvenile 14 years or older who used a gun in any felony.

- A juvenile arrested on a warrant.

- A juvenile who committed crimes if any of the following are included:

> The juvenile lacks proper and effective parental guidance.
>
> The juvenile is destitute or lacking the necessities of home.
>
> The juvenile's residence is deemed unfit.
>
> The juvenile is a danger to the public because of a mental or physical disability.

PEER PRESSURE

So many times I hear teenagers say that they are not in a gang but their friends are. If your friends are in a gang and you hang with them, guess what, you are in a gang. When I was young, some of my friends encouraged me to shoplift and fight or do something wrong, but I can't remember any of them encouraging me to stay in school or go to class.

Parents, it is important to know your child's friends. I have had parents tell me that their child is missing or has run away from home. When I ask them if they can tell me who their child's friends are or where they live, they can't. Juvenile offenders rarely commit crimes by themselves. Gangs are nothing more than a group of friends banding together to commit criminal acts. One of the hardest lessons to teach children is that sometimes their friends are not really their friends. It takes tremendous courage to leave the group. Our children need to be taught to choose their friends wisely. No friend is worth your freedom. You have to keep this in mind at all times.

Many juveniles enrolled in high school allowed negative peer pressure to influence them into committing crimes and they are currently serving long prison sentences. They will never graduate on a high school stage. The simple pleasures that we all take for granted are gone inside a prison. The juvenile cannot get up in the middle of the night and go to the refrigerator to get a snack. Since he chose to hang with certain "friends" and commit crime, now the juvenile justice system tells him when to get up and when to go to bed. Where are those friends now? It's just a matter of time before they become tired of visiting you and sending you money. Friends aren't going to do the time. Parents must impress upon their children that the type of friends they choose will have a direct impact on the quality of their lives.

GANGS

Gangs are a major factor why our children do not graduate from high school. In the Los Angeles County there are approximately 300,000 gang members. Very few ever complete high school. The effects of gang violence, whether psychological or physical, are long lasting on its members. Some youth gangs were formed as immigrant children in impoverished areas began to band together as an informal type of youth social club; others were formed by inner city youth. They committed petty crimes and fought with juveniles from other neighborhoods. Their most dangerous weapon was a "switch blade knife." The gangs were a small part of the community and they were romanticized in plays and movies like "Westside Story." Although these were youth street gangs, they were not the modern day violent street gangs that exist in all urban and rural cities across America today. These gangs were considered juvenile delinquents and labeled "dropouts" or the "kids that would not amount to much." In the early 1970s, gangs took on a more territorial nature and became more violent.

In the 1980s, with the emergence of crack cocaine (a cheap and highly addictive form of cocaine), gang membership greatly increased. Crack cocaine was the vehicle gangs used to buy guns, cars, and jewelry. This fast money lifestyle appealed to many of the youth who felt shut out from the American Dream and saw no other way out of their impoverished conditions. The gangs grew and the death bath of the 1980s cost the lives of thousands of young people fighting over "turf" and the right to sell drugs in the community.

Some street gangs have even been linked to prison gangs, doing their bidding in the neighborhood. Although the police began an aggressive campaign to fight gang violence, it did not slow down the growth of gangs or violence. In the 1980s, it seemed as though the news media was reporting a gang related murder or drive-by shooting every day. With the proceeds from illegal drugs, gang members were able to purchase sophisticated weapons, including such items as AK47 assault rifles and automatic and semi-automatic handguns. A 14 year old child carrying an assault rifle with a pocketful of money and drugs proved a volatile combination. The rise of violent street gangs increased and neither the police department nor the juvenile justice system was prepared for this new type of youthful offender.

Gang growth and violence continued to escalate well into the 1990s. Juvenile crime has since decreased but gang membership remains at a very high level. The average age of a youth gang member is between the ages of 14 and 25. Many of the juveniles incarcerated are there because of drugs and gang involvement.

FEMALE OFFENDERS

When we imagine a juvenile offender, we usually think of a hard looking male "gang banger"; but that is simply not the case. As the crime rate of males increased, so did the crime rate of females. Their crimes became more violent. Many times the police officers would not search girls as thoroughly as they would search males, so girls were used to carry contraband. Many girls think that the juvenile justice system will not deal with them as harshly as their male counterpart. This is a false conception as the juvenile justice system does deal harshly with females that commit crimes.

Our young girls face issues of low self-esteem, teen pregnancy, and lack of parental supervision, which all play a role in them becoming involved in gangs or criminal activity. Girls need to see their mothers in nurturing relationships to give them examples of what type of men they want in their lives. Parents, watch your daughters carefully because if you don't, someone else will.

PARENTAL RESPONSIBILILITY

Parenting is a huge responsibility. Parents of minors are responsible for the behavior of their children. Many times when young people go to jail there is a direct relationship between the behavior of the child and the way the child was raised. Parents have a natural tendency to protect and defend their children. When parents defend the negative behavior of their children, they do a terrible disservice to them. Some parents display negative behavior in front of their children which encourages the negative behaviors that lead to their child's future involvement with the juvenile justice system.

If the school contacts you about your child's behavior, come to the school as promptly as you can. Be a good listener. Listen to what everyone has to say including your child. Do not arrive at the school and use profanity with the school administrator. The school can be your greatest ally. Most schools offer some form of counseling free of charge to the students. Teachers, principals, counselors, college counselors, school nurses, and school police are all there to offer support and make sure that your adolescent is successful. Get familiar with the staff who works at your child's school. You will be glad that you did. When teachers and counselors see that you are taking an active part in your child's schooling, they will pay much more attention to your child.

THE ROLE OF THE FATHER

There is a saying that speaks about the sins of the father being passed to the son and that the process continues generation after generation. This applies to many of the young people involved in the juvenile justice system today. Many of the juvenile offenders incarcerated had a parent or immediate family member in jail. Many of the gang members on the street today are second and third generation gang members.

Addressing this issue is not easy and I don't claim to possess all of the answers to such a complex problem. I do know that education breaks all barriers and the more our young people are educated, the better they will be at dealing with and avoiding the generational pitfalls of their parents. Essential information must be instilled in the child by the parent or role model that is not involved in negative behavior. The child must be taught that it is all right to love a parent and disagree with her actions or lifestyle. For example, if the father is a gang member, love him but separate your love of him from his criminal activity.

Unless someone instills a sense of right and wrong in our children, they will likely copy negative behavior. I have heard of juveniles being arrested and making the statement, "I'm like this and so were my father and his father." The role of the father is crucial in the proper development of our children. Studies have proven that when the father is not a positive role model for the child, it increases the chances of that child being involved in the juvenile justice system.

WARNING SIGNS

Warning signs are the behavior patterns that most youth exhibit prior to committing a crime. These signs are not universal and sometimes children without any signs commit crimes, but there are usually indicators. We know that young people who live in a single parent home have more problems than young people with two active parents. They have a strike against them from very early in their lives. We also know that teenage pregnancy has a negative effect on the teenager and the newborn.

Poor school behavior is yet another excellent indication of trouble ahead. A child who is constantly having discipline problems at school is a child headed for trouble. Poor school grades are also a warning sign. A youth who has poor grades has a greater potential for getting into trouble for a variety of reasons. Whenever a child drops out of school, her chances of becoming involved in criminal activity shoot through the roof. The vast majority of adult prisoners never completed high school and read at an elementary school level if they can read at all.

Negative friends and bad associations have landed many young people in a juvenile facility. If your child is hanging out with the wrong crowd of friends and you do not stop him immediately, you are opening the door for criminal behavior. Remember a gang is nothing more than a group of friends involved in negative behavior. Loss of parental control is the most crucial and dangerous warning sign. Once a child openly disrespects or abuses his parents, he has probably already exhibited some of the other warning signs. Without immediate intervention, this child is guaranteed to become involved in the juvenile justice system at some point in his adolescent life.

CRIME PREVENTION

Many elements are involved in eradicating juvenile crime. Parent involvement is at the top of that list. Children need the love that only a parent or guardian can provide. Once you send a child out into the world, you have little control over her actions. All you can do is pray that the values you have instilled will outweigh the negative peer pressure he will face. I realize some of the difficult circumstances that parents find themselves in trying to raise children today, but love does not cost anything.

Show your children you love them by getting involved in their lives. Activity is also a key to fighting gang involvement. When young people are involved in some type of activity, such as baseball or basketball, their self-esteem increases and they meet others who will have a positive influence on their lives. Whether it is sports, academics or the arts, get your children away from the television and computer and involve them in productive activities. I started in the martial arts when I was 14. I remember going home after practice too tired and sore to think about getting into trouble.

EXAMPLES OF CRIME

Many times juveniles are arrested for things they did not know were crimes or they did not know the severity of the crime they committed. Unfortunately, ignorance is no excuse of the law. Listed below is a group of scenarios describing crimes committed at schools. **Note:** Crimes committed against school employees carry additional penalties.

Scenario #1

One student watches another student talking on a cell phone. That student runs up behind the other student, grabs the cell phone and takes off running. If that student is caught he will be charged with **Grand Theft Person** or **Robbery,** both of which are felony crimes.

Scenario #2

One student gets mad at another student and tells the other student "I'm going to kill you after school." If the student who was threatened felt in fear of her life and the student who made the threat had the means to carry it out, she can be charged with **Threat,** a misdemeanor crime.

Scenario #3

Pocket check is what the older students call checking the pockets of younger students' pants for money. This is **Robbery,** a felony crime.

Scenario #4

Students in the lunch area decide to have a food fight. A student throws an apple and hits another student in the head. The student can be charged with **Battery,** a misdemeanor crime.

TYPES OF OFFENSES

Infractions: Crimes that require a fine when there is a guilty verdict.

Misdemeanor: Crimes that require a fine or up to six months to a year or both. A juvenile cannot be sentenced for longer than one year for any misdemeanor.

Felony: Various types of felonies require incarceration, a fine, or both. Depending on the type of felony, a juvenile can be sentenced and not released until the age of 25.

CATEGORIES OF CRIMES

Violent Crimes: Crimes which are perpetrated on a person, including homicide, rape, and battery.

Property Crimes: Crimes committed with the intent of gaining property through the use or threat of force against a person.

Drug-Related Crimes: Possession or sale of illegal narcotics, or manufacturing illegal substances.

Crimes can fall in one category or a combination of all the above.

CRIMES COMMITTED BY JUVENILES

Assault: Unlawful attempt, joined with the ability to commit a violent injury on another (In California it must be joined with the crime of Battery).

Assault with a Deadly Weapon (ADW): Assault with an instrument other than a firearm, or by a means of force likely to produce great bodily injury against another person.

Battery: Any willful and unlawful use of force on the person of another.

Burglary: Entry into a residence, room, or any structure, tent, vessel, railroad, car, cargo, container, trailer, coach, inhabited camper, locked vehicle, aircraft, mine, etc., with the intent to commit grand or petty larceny or to commit a felony.

Disturbing the Peace: Fighting or challenging to fight a person(s), in a public place.

Grand Theft: Value over $400 in money, labor, real or personal property.

Grand Theft Person: Felony taking of personal property that is in the possession or immediate presence of another, and against that person's will.

Kidnapping: Taking away a person against his or her will.

Knife on School Grounds: Bringing to or possession of a weapon on school grounds: a dirk, dagger, ice pick, knife with a blade over ½ inch long, locking folding knife, razor with unguarded blade, tazer or stun gun, pellet, BB, or spot marker gun, on school grounds of, or within a Kindergarten through 12th grade public or private school.

Minor in possession of a Firearm: Unlawful for a person under the age of 18 to possess a firearm (unless in certain supervised or sporting situations).

Murder: Unlawful killing of a human being, or a fetus, with malice aforethought.

Noise: Maliciously and willfully disturbing another person by loud and unreasonable noise.

Criminal Threat: Threaten death or great bodily injury with the specific intent that the verbal, written, or electronic device statement is taken as a threat, even if the person had no intention to carry out the threat or if it were not possible under the current circumstances. If the person who was threatened can convey that he expected an immediate and specific execution of the threat, according to the law, it is considered a legitimate threat.

Rape: An act of sexual intercourse with a person against her will by force, violence, duress, menace, or fear of immediate and unlawful bodily injury on the victim or other person.

Robbery: The taking of someone's property accomplished by force or fear.

Vandalism: When a person intentionally damages or defaces private or public property.

Voluntary manslaughter: Killing a human being in which the offender has no prior intent to kill and acted during "the heat of passion."

JUVENILE OFFENDERS

Juvenile offenders are usually placed into four main categories depending on the nature and seriousness of the crimes committed.

Informal Probation: Juveniles convicted of minor offenses. The probation officer can place the juvenile under informal probation and assist the juvenile with services for substance abuse, mental health, shelter, and other services.

Status Offender: Juveniles that have committed offenses unique to juveniles and not adults. Two examples are truancy and curfew violations. The status offender can be placed on formal probation.

Criminal Offenders: Juveniles charged with a misdemeanor or felony. They can be placed on formal probation and placed in juvenile facilities prior to their case (petition) being adjudicated (tried). If their petition is sustained (guilty/convicted) in a juvenile court, they can be incarcerated in juvenile hall, camp, or a state juvenile facility.

Juvenile Remanded to Superior Court: Juveniles that will be tried as adults. Any juvenile age 16 or 17 who commits one of a number of felonies, or juveniles aged 14 or older (in some states 11), who are convicted of murder get sentenced to either a state juvenile facility or state prison.

JUVENILE DEFINITIONS

Adjudication Hearing: The term for the procedure in which a juvenile is tried for the offense for which they are accused.

Aftercare: Another term for parole or probation.

Arrest: Procedure when a person officially accused of a crime is taken into police custody. Suspect (adult), Subject (juvenile).

Cite-Back: A form used to instruct parents to return to the police station for further investigation when a juvenile is arrested and released to parents.

Detention: When a juvenile is held in custody prior to the court appearance.

Disposition: The punishment for being found guilty of the crime.

Gladys R: A form that must be completed prior to arresting juveniles under 14 to determine if they know right from wrong.

Inmate: Term for incarcerated adult.

Juvenile: A person under the age of 18 who is charged with a criminal act.

Juvenile Hall: Detention facility used to house juveniles prior to court hearing or sentencing.

Minor: A person under the age of 21 years old.

Probation: When a minor receives a specific set of rules to be carried out rather than incarceration. The probation is ordered by the court and enforced by a probation officer.

Subject: A person under the age of 18 accused of committing a crime.

Suspect: A person over the age of 18 accused of a crime.

Ward: Term used for minors for whom the courts have taken responsibility over. Incarcerated juveniles are considered wards. Incarcerated adults are called inmates.

CODES OF LAW RELATING TO JUVENILES

Welfare and Institution Codes are sections of the law that involve minors.

Penal Code are laws relating to crimes and offenses and the penalty received for violating them.

Health and Safety Codes are laws used regarding minors use or possession of tobacco, drugs and paraphernalia.

AFTERTHOUGHT

I remember when I was a young man failing in high school and on the verge of dropping out. I remember a young man I loved who had everything to live for but fell victim to a juvenile with a gun. I remember the promises I made to my teachers at Central YMCA High School in Chicago; that I would do everything I could to help young people when I became an adult, because they had helped me when I was a teenager. If this book can help one overwhelmed parent caught in a system that would rather build prisons than schools or if it makes one youth think about the consequences of juvenile crime, I will have repaid my teachers.